Now You Are Seven

Now You Are Seven A Birthday Book

Edited by Alison M. Abel

Illustrated by Sarah Hale

RAND McNALLY & COMPANY
Chicago · New York · San Francisco

Published in the U.S.A.
by Rand McNally & Company 1973
ISBN 0-528-82194-6

© Ward Lock Limited London 1973

First published in Great Britain 1973 by Ward Lock
Limited, 116 Baker Street, London, W1M 2BB.

Text filmset in 14pt Apollo
by Yendall & Company Ltd, London.

Printed and bound in Belgium
by Casterman S.A., Tournai.

CONTENTS

Prince Brian's Tasks

One morning, in the spring of the year, Mr. Flanagan, the famous singing leprechaun, was sitting under an elm tree in the forest when he met a prince called Brian.

Brian was riding through the land seeking fame and fortune. When he saw Mr. Flanagan sitting there he called out: 'Excuse me, sir, I am Prince Brian, and I'm riding through the land seeking fame and fortune. Can you tell me where I might find them?'

Mr. Flanagan thought for a moment, then he sang his reply:

'There lives a princess close at hand
And she's the fairest in the land.
Of riches she has quite a lot,
But a husband she has not.'

'Good gracious,' thought Brian. 'This must be Mr. Flanagan, the famous singing leprechaun!' But before he could think another thought the little man sang on:

'Yes, Mr. Flanagan is my name,
And singing is my game.
Prince Brian I will gladly aid,
And see his fortune made.'

Brian was, of course, delighted to hear this, and following the leprechaun's directions he set off at once for the Princess's castle. As soon as the Prince and Princess met they fell in love. They would have been married right away, but the King – the Princess's father – had made a rule that whoever wished to marry his

6

daughter would first have to complete three very difficult tasks. The tasks were so difficult that no one had yet managed to complete them all, though three hundred and thirty-four people had tried.

'Before you marry my daughter,' the King said, 'you must bring to me a golden egg from a nest of fire.'

Brian went off at once to see Mr. Flanagan, for the leprechaun had promised to help him. 'I think he means a dragon's egg,' Brian explained to his friend. 'But where on earth will I find one? I didn't think there were any dragons left in Ireland.'

Mr. Flanagan sang his reply:

'There is a dragon that I know,
He lives far in the West;
And he has lots of golden eggs,
Down in his fiery nest.
He wouldn't give his golden eggs
To any mortal man;
So tell him that you're needing one
For your old friend Flanagan.'

Brian rode off to the West and soon found the dragon's nest.

'Excuse me,' he called out. 'Are you at home, Mr. Dragon, sir?' Brian thought it best to be very polite to a dragon.

There was a great roar, and smoke and flames shot out from inside the nest.

'Who are you and what do you want?' The dragon sounded angry.

'I'm very sorry to disturb you,' Brian said, 'but Mr. Flanagan sent me to ask if you had a golden egg you could spare him?'

'Why on earth didn't you say so!' the dragon laughed. 'For Mr. Flanagan — anything. Are you sure that one egg will be enough?'

Brian took the egg and rode as fast as he could back to the palace. The King was surprised to see him back so soon. Few had managed to complete this task, and none with apparently so little effort.

'Next,' he said to Brian, 'you must find for me a golden fish with silver fins swimming in an emerald pool.'

Brian was dismayed. He had no idea at all where to find such a fish. So back he went to the forest to find his leprechaun friend. Mr. Flanagan listened attentively to his story. Then, without so much as a pause for thought, he sang:

'There is a giant that I know,
His name is Finn McCool;
And golden fish with silver fins
Swim in his emerald pool.

He'd never give his golden fish
To any mortal man,
So tell him that it's needed by
His old friend Flanagan.'

Brian set out at break of day for Finn McCool's castle, which was in the far north of Ireland. The giant was very tall—nearly twenty-three and a half feet (without his boots on) and Brian was still a long way off when Finn McCool saw him coming.

The giant stood by the front gate of his castle and bellowed: 'Who are you, little man, and how dare you come so near to my castle?'

When the giant shouted he caused such a strong wind that trees were uprooted and blown for miles across the countryside and cows and horses were tossed in the air. Luckily Brian was just out of reach of the blast, but even so he had to hold on tightly to a nearby oak tree to prevent himself from being blown away.

'I'm sorry if I'm trespassing, Mr. McCool, but my friend Mr. Flanagan, the leprechaun, sent me to ask if you could possibly spare him one of your golden fish?'

'Mr. Flanagan, is it?' the giant said, and he laughed. Although it was quite a friendly laugh, the wind it made blew all the leaves off Brian's oak tree, and very nearly blew him away, too. 'If it's for Mr. Flanagan, you can have twenty fish. Just hang on there, my lad, and I'll get them for you.'

Brian assured the giant that one would be sufficient, and soon he was riding back to the King's castle with the fish in a beautiful emerald bowl balanced carefully in front of him.

When Brian reached the King's palace this time, the King was even more amazed to see him. No one had ever got this far with the tasks before. He was half inclined to let Brian off the third task and allow him to marry the Princess right away. But no, he thought. Rules are rules, and the third task must be completed.

'Prince, you are a very brave man,' he said. 'But before you can marry my daughter you must bring to me the many-colored O'Tingley-bird.'

When Brian got back to the forest and Mr. Flanagan he was very, very gloomy.

'How on earth can I find a bird like that?' he moaned. 'I've never even heard

of it! I doubt if such a bird exists. I may as well forget my Princess and go back home.'

But Mr. Flanagan was not the least bit dismayed. He winked, took a deep breath, and sang:

> 'The O'Tingley-bird is very rare,
> In fact there's only one;
> He lives away down in the South
> Near the mountains of Kildon.
> He'll never leave his forest home
> For any mortal man,
> So tell him that he's needed by
> His old friend Flanagan.'

Needless to say, Brian was delighted, and he set off for the Kildon mountains straight away. It was about five in the afternoon when he got there, and without

further ado he called out for the O'Tingley-bird. There was a sudden flapping of wings and the most beautiful bird you ever saw fluttered to the ground. Its feathers were a whole patchwork of the most lovely colors—all the colors of the rainbow.

Brian explained to the O'Tingley-bird why he had come. The O'Tingley-bird scratched his head and thought for a moment. Then he spoke.

'You know, Brian, I have been getting a bit bored with living all alone in this forest, and a change is as good as a rest, so they say. And if I can go and live alongside the famous Mr. Flanagan, nothing could make me happier. I'll come with you, Brian, that I will.'

So off they went and in no time at all they arrived back at the King's palace.

10

This time Brian was greeted by people cheering and flags and banners waving, and all the bells ringing. The King gave his consent for the wedding, and Brian and his Princess were married the very next day. After the wedding Brian and the Princess took the O'Tingley-bird to see Mr. Flanagan in the forest.

'Mr. Flanagan,' said Brian, 'how can I ever thank you enough for everything you've done for me?'

And this was Mr. Flanagan's reply:

Be happy and make others happy,
Be jolly and laughing and gay;
Be peaceful and make others peaceful,
And let music fill every day.
When I hear the whole land a-singing,
Every child, every woman and man;
When the mountains with music are
    ringing,
You'll have pleased Mr. Flanagan.'

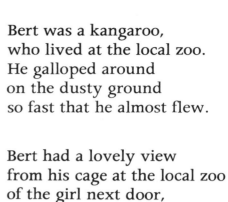

BERT

Bert was a kangaroo,
who lived at the local zoo.
He galloped around
on the dusty ground
so fast that he almost flew.

Bert had a lovely view
from his cage at the local zoo
of the girl next door,
who was five foot four,
and she was a kangaroo too.

Bert loved this kangaroo
(whose name was Betsy Lou).
He was deeply entranced
with the way that she pranced
in the shimmering morning dew.

Bert cried to Betsy Lou:
'Oh, let me be married to you!'
So they lived in one cage
till a very old age
and died at ninety-two.

A DAY AT THE ZOO

Have you ever been to the zoo? If you haven't, why not ask your parents to take you the next time you are planning a day's outing? If there isn't one close to your home, perhaps there will be one nearby when you go on vacation.

All zoos are fun, of course, but the best ones to visit are those where many of the animals roam around in the open air, separated from the visitors only by a fence or low wall. Animals which live outside are much happier and healthier than those in cages—and they smell better, too!

When you visit the zoo look out for the notices telling you when feeding times are. Usually different kinds of animals are fed at different times, so you should be able to see several zoo meals during your visit. The lions and tigers can be quite frightening as they roar and leap on-to chunks of raw meat. You will soon be reminded that those cuddly cats you saw lazily sunning themselves a few minutes ago are really fierce and dangerous wild animals.

The seals really enjoy feeding time—and not just for the fish they are given. To them it is a chance to show off their elegance and cleverness as they catch the fish the keeper throws to them.

The apes and monkeys are up to all sorts of tricks at meal-times. You may even find them enjoying a lively little tea-party, with doll-sized cups and saucers—and shocking table manners!

A word of warning. Never feed the animals at the zoo yourself, not even if they ask for food. The food you give them

could make them ill. Even if you are sure you have the right food for them you must remember that the animals in a zoo are wild animals, however gentle and pretty they may look. You could get badly hurt if one of them struck out at you, or decided you would taste better than a bit of stale bun.

You will probably want to take some photographs of the animals while you are at the zoo. If you are good at drawing, you could take a sketch pad and pencil with you. It is very difficult to remember exactly what an animal looks like; but when you have one in front of you you can check up on just what kind of ears and eyes it has, and how long its legs and body are. It is a good idea to take a notebook with you, too. Then, as you come to each animal, you can read the notice on the railings and make notes about which part of the world it comes from, and any other interesting facts. When you get home, you could make a chart – or even better, draw a map – and illustrate each country with pictures of the animals that are found there.

You will learn a lot about animals, birds and fishes from a trip to the zoo, as well as having lots of fun. Next time you go, see if you can find out the answers to the Zoo Quiz on page 15. If you can't tell the answers from looking at the animals or reading the notices, you can ask one of the keepers to help you.

ZOO QUIZ

1. Which elephant has the biggest ears, the African elephant or the Indian elephant?

2. What is the biggest living animal?

3. How big is a baby kangaroo when it is first born?

4. What has sharp claws, donkey-like ears, a very long tongue and a pig-like face?

5. Where in the frozen North do penguins live?

6. What is the smallest living mammal?

7. What is the slowest animal in the world and where does it live?

8. What is the largest flying bird and what is its wing span?

9. What animal spends all its life eating the leaves of the eucalyptus tree?

10. What is the name of the largest living lizard and where does it live?

11. Name six members of the cat family.

12. What animal plays dead when danger threatens?

(Answers: page 28)

GAMES TO PLAY AT YOUR PARTY

Here are some ideas for games to play at your party.

STATUES

One player is chosen as Mr. Sculptor. He stands at one end of the room with his face to the wall. The other players creep up behind him. When Mr. Sculptor suddenly turns round they must stand quite still and not move until he turns away again. Anyone who moves while Mr. Sculptor is watching them is out of the game. The first player to touch Mr. Sculptor is the winner and becomes the next Mr. Sculptor.

NOSE IN THE MATCHBOX

All you need to play this game is two empty matchbox covers. Divide your guests into two teams. The teams stand in two lines facing each other. The leaders stand at the head of each team with the empty matchbox covers fixed to their noses. The idea is to pass the matchbox from nose to nose right down the team. No player must touch the matchbox with his hands—if he does, the matchbox is passed back to the leader, and his side begins all over again.

BURST THE BAG

For this game you will need as many paper bags of the same size as there are players. Divide the paper bags into two equal heaps and put them at one end of the room. The players are divided into two teams and stand in lines at the other end of the room. At the word 'Go', the first one from each team runs across the room, picks up a paper bag, blows it up, and bursts it. Then he runs back to his team and touches the next player. This player then runs to burst a bag, returns to his team, and touches the third player; and so on. The first team to burst all its paper bags is the winner.

The Old Man is Always Right

There was once an old peasant who lived with his wife in a little old farmhouse. They did not have many possessions, but they did have one thing which was very useful to them, and that was their horse. Nevertheless the peasant and his wife decided it would be best to sell the horse, or to exchange it for something that would be of even more use to them.

'The fair is coming to the town today,' said the wife. 'Why don't you sell our horse there, or perhaps exchange it for something more useful? You will know what it is best to do.'

So the old man set off on the horse toward the town. He had not gone far before he met a man driving a cow. It was as nice a cow as one could wish to see.

'She would give beautiful milk,' thought the old peasant. 'I could not do better than to exchange my horse for that cow. You with the cow!' he called. 'Stop a minute. Will you exchange your cow for my horse?'

The owner of the cow agreed, and the exchange was made.

The old peasant might as well have turned back home, for he had done all he had to do. But he decided he would go on toward the fair that he had made a start.

Soon he came up to a man with a sheep. It was a very good sheep, fat, and with a fine fleece.

'I should dearly like that sheep,'

thought the old peasant. 'It could eat the grass on the roadside, and in the winter we could have it in the house. It would be better in many ways to have a sheep than a cow. Shall we exchange?' he said to the man.

The man agreed, the exchange was made, and the peasant and his sheep went on towards the fair.

Before long he met a man coming out of a field carrying a goose under his arm.

'That's a nice plump goose you have there,' said the old peasant. 'It would be just the thing for my wife. She has always wanted a goose. Shall we exchange?'

The owner of the goose was willing enough, and the old peasant got the goose.

By this time he had nearly reached the town. By the side of the road was a potato field, and in the field was a hen. It was a very fine-looking hen.

The moment the old peasant saw the hen he cried: 'That's the very finest hen I ever saw in my life! How I should like to have that hen. Shall we exchange?' he

said to the farmer who was picking potatoes in the field.

The farmer agreed, and took the old peasant's goose, while the peasant took the hen.

By now the peasant was feeling tired and hungry as well as thirsty, so he made his way to an inn on the edge of the town. As he was going in he met a serving-man carrying a heavy sack.

'What have you got in your sack?' asked the old peasant.

'Apples,' said the man. 'Windfalls for the pigs.'

'For the pigs? What a waste!' cried the old peasant. 'We had only one apple on our tree last year. "Now there's riches," my old woman used to say. What would she say to a whole sackful?'

'What will you give me for them?' asked the man.

'I'll give you my hen,' replied the old peasant. And so he did.

He carried the apples into the inn and set down the sack against the stove. The

room was filled with people on their way to the fair. Among them were two strangers, so rich that their pockets were almost bursting with gold pieces.

'*Hiss! Hiss!*'

There was a fire in the stove, and the apples were beginning to roast!

'What is that noise?' cried the guests.

'Why, I'll tell you,' said the old peasant, moving away his sack of apples. And he told them about all the exchanges he had made on the road.

'My word, you'll be in trouble when you get home!' said one of the strangers. 'What will your wife do when she hears about it?'

'What will she do?' cried the peasant. 'She'll give me a kiss, and she'll say: "What my old man does is always right".'

The strangers laughed.

'I'll bet you a sack of gold to a sack of apples that she won't,' said one.

The peasant readily agreed to the wager. The innkeeper brought out his cart, the peasant and the two strangers got in, and off they went to the old farmhouse.

The wife was standing waiting at the door.

'I've made the exchange,' the old peasant told her.

'Trust you to know what you are about,' said the old woman, smiling, and noticing neither the two strangers nor the sack of apples.

'I exchanged the horse for a cow,' said the old man.

'Heaven be praised!' cried the wife. 'Why, now we shall have fresh milk and butter and cheese to eat.'

'Yes, but I changed the cow for a sheep.'

'Better and better,' said the old woman. 'A sheep will give us wool. I shall have plenty of warm stockings this winter. A cow is of no use for stockings.'

'Yes, but I changed the sheep for a goose.'

'Then we shall really taste roast goose before the year is out! You must have done that on purpose to please me,' cried the old woman.

19

'Yes, but I changed the goose for a hen.'

'An excellent exchange, too! She will lay eggs, and we shall have chickens. How I have longed to have some chickens!'

'Yes, but I exchanged the hen for a sack of windfall apples.'

'Apples!' cried the wife. 'Why, what do you think? As soon as you were gone this morning I began to wonder what I could make for your supper. At last I thought of ham and pancakes. I had the eggs, and I had the ham, but I had no sweet herbs. So I went across to the schoolmaster's, for I know they have plenty. But his wife is a mean woman.

"Lend you some herbs?" she said. "Oh, we have nothing in our garden to lend. I could not even lend you a green apple, my dear woman." And now I can lend her a whole sackful of apples!'

The wife gave her husband a hearty kiss. 'What my old man does is always right,' she said.

'Well done!' cried the strangers. 'And good luck to you both. It is worth the money any day to see you.'

And they paid down a bushel of gold coins to the old man whose wife believed that he was always right, and gave him a kiss instead of a scolding.

DIVING TO DISCOVERY

Man's attempts to fly began nearly five hundred years ago, when Leonardo da Vinci made models and drawings of the first flying machine. Experiments continued through the centuries, until today man has been so successful that not only can he fly across the world in a matter of hours, but astronauts have even been thousands of miles into space and walked on the surface of the moon.

Yet exploration of the oceans has only been possible in the past twenty years or so, since Jacques-Yves Cousteau invented the aqualung in 1943. The sea covers nearly three-quarters (71%) of the earth's surface, and the average depth of the great oceans is 11,811 feet, while the average height of the land is only 2,493 feet. So you can see that until recently there was a vast area of our planet about which we knew very little.

Now, with the help of the aqualung, divers can see and study at first hand the fantastic and beautiful range of animal and plant life under the sea. Their discoveries help us to build up a more complete picture of the world in which we live.

What we learn about life under the sea is also helping scientists to work out ways of farming the ocean. With more and more people living on earth, and space for farming on the land always decreasing as more homes and roads and factories are built, food from the sea could well be an important part of our diet in the future.

Underwater exploration is not only helping us to understand the life of the

sea and to plan the future; it is also helping us to learn how men have lived in the past. Underwater archaeologists are now exploring the remains of ancient cities which centuries ago were submerged by the sea. Off the coast of Greece in particular, important new discoveries are being made beneath the sea which help historians to understand more about the ancient world and the people who once lived in these sunken cities.

PATTERNS WITH PAINTS

These patterned papers are easy to do and make pretty pictures to put on the wall. You could use them for wrapping birthday and Christmas presents, too, and make a card to match. Or you could cover a scrap-book with a paper of your own design.

POTATO PRINTS

You will need a large, smooth potato, a felt-tip pen, some paint in a shallow dish, and a sheet of paper. Cut the potato in half. Dry the inside of the potato by pressing it on a piece of newspaper. With the felt-tip pen, draw the outline of the shape you want to print on the potato. Now cut away the potato round the outline so that the shape is raised about a quarter of an inch. Dip the potato in the paint and then press it firmly on to the paper. Cover the paper

22

with prints of the shape in a pattern that you like. If you want to use two colors, use two potatoes, so that the paints don't mix.

CANDLE DRAWINGS

Draw your pattern on the paper with a white wax candle. Now wash over the paper with paint. The paint will not stick to the wax, and the pattern you have drawn will appear in white.

SPRAY PAINTING

You will need an old toothbrush, some paints, and a shape to spray round. The shape could be a picture of a bird, fish, flower or animal cut from a magazine. Or you can use a flat leaf to make a pattern like this one.

Mix the paint in a jar. Spread the paper on the table and put the leaf on the paper. Weight it down in the middle so that it will stay quite still. Dip the toothbrush bristles in the paint, and carefully spray the paint around the leaf.

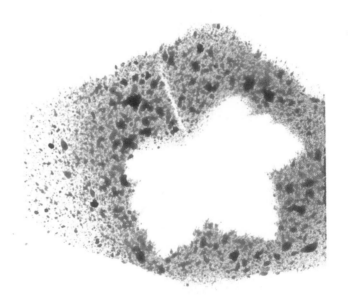

ANIMALS AT WORK

Men have used animals to help them in their work since the earliest times. Today each working animal is specially bred for the job it has to do.

Dogs are said to be man's oldest friend, and they were probably the first animal to be tamed by him. Later, different types of dog were bred, each type suited to the kind of work it had to do. Bulldogs, with their thick-set necks and strong jaws and teeth, were used many years ago in the sport of bull-baiting. St. Bernards and Newfoundlands were used for rescue work. Today most dogs are kept as pets,

but some still have important jobs to do. The sheepdog helps the shepherd look after the sheep. Huskies and terriers are used for pulling sledges, and retrievers and terriers in hunting and shooting. The police use highly trained dogs for tracking criminals. Guide dogs, which have the important job of helping the blind travel safely, even in busy cities, are carefully chosen and trained for their work.

Horses, too, have been helping men in their work for many thousands of years. Like dogs, horses have also been bred to suit the work they have to do. The race horse is built for speed, and is very slim and streamlined. Hunters must be able to cover great distances as well as move quickly, so they are built much more solidly, with stronger legs than the race horse. Cart horses are specially bred for their great pulling strength.

Some animals are already built to suit the conditions in which they live. This means that men have not needed to breed them specially for the work they do. Camels, for instance, have large padded feet so that they can walk easily over sandy surfaces. They have humps which store fat on which they can feed, so they can go without food for long periods. They can also live without water for several days. Because of this, camels are very useful as beasts of burden in the desert. They are used by traders to carry loads across the dry, sandy Sahara Desert, the plains of Mongolia and Siberia, and the desert regions of Australia.

Johnny Appleseed

This is the story of a man with a heart of gold who lived in America almost two hundred years ago. In those days people were only just beginning to go westward, inland from the colonies of New England where they had first settled. Had you traveled west with these pioneers in their wagons, you would have found a wild and unfriendly country, open grassland and thick forest inhabited only by animals and Indian tribes, with here and there a log cabin where new settlers were trying to grow corn and potatoes.

You might also have met John Chapman, the hero of this story. If you had, you would have thought him a strange figure indeed, tramping along a forest path, barefooted except in the very coldest weather. He would be wearing an ill-fitting sack with holes cut out for his arms and legs and, on his head, the tin pan in which he cooked his food. He carried no weapons as other travelers did. Instead, on his back, he had a large bag full of apple seeds.

John Chapman had once lived on the East Coast in Massachusetts where there were plenty of farms nestling peacefully among the apple orchards: orchards heavy with pink and white blossom in the spring and rosy red apples in the late summer. One day, when he was sitting in the sun eating an apple, John thought of the pioneers tramping westward across new country. How much more friendly and comfortable their scattered farms would seem if they were surrounded by apple trees! So he gave up his own home

to a poor woman who had a large family, and collected a sack of apple seeds from the cider mill. Then he, too, set off westward into Ohio, planting his seeds wherever he went and giving a small bagful to everyone he met. It wasn't long before he was known among the pioneers as 'Johnny Appleseed'.

John loved nothing better than to be out in the open air, following the wagon trails. He called at the scattered log cabins to chat with the settlers, and brought small gifts for their children. He would stop and help the families to clear their land for corn. They were glad when he sat by their fireside in the evening, for their lives were lonely and the news that he brought was the only news they had. John believed that as well as scattering his apple seeds, he must also preach the Christian gospel. As he sat with a family in the evenings, he would read to them from the Bible.

When he had used up all his seeds, John would go back to the East and get more from the cider mills. Then he set out

26

again to cross the Middle West. As he wandered about he grew to know the animals—deer, wolves and foxes—and the many kinds of birds. A mother bear would let him play with her cubs because she knew he would not harm them; he never feared a bite from a poisonous snake on his bare feet. He came to know the Indians, too, and gave them herbs for medicines so that they grew to love him and showed him their secret trails, even when they were fighting other white men.

Once the Indians saved his life. The winter had been long and more severe than usual; Johnny Appleseed was afraid that the apple trees he was planting would die. He himself became weak and ill and collapsed in the snow. There he was

found by an Indian tribe who took him to their village where they cared for him and nursed him back to health.

Johnny Appleseed hated war and fighting. He thought that all men should love one another and live together as brothers. He tried always to make peace between the white settlers and the Indians. In the war of 1812, when the Indians fought against the settlers in the West, they never stopped John from wandering through their territory, and he would often carry a warning word to the settlers that an Indian attack was on its way.

So the years passed by, and the apples seeded and grew into trees. As the country became more populated, and small towns took the place of lone settlers' farms, Johnny Appleseed went farther west still with the pioneers out on the frontier. Today there are hundreds of acres of land in Ohio, Indiana and parts of Illinois which are thick with trees, now grown large and old, but still covered every year with blossoms and apples, each in its own season. And these trees were grown from the seeds carried on the back of Johnny Appleseed, a true lover of his fellow men who all his life put the welfare and comfort of others before that of himself.

Zoo Quiz Answers

1. The African elephant; 2. Blue whale. Remember the whale is a mammal, not a fish; 3. About the size of your little finger; 4. Aardvark of Africa; 5. Nowhere as penguins only live in the Antarctic; 6. Etruscan shrew, which is under 3 inches long, including its tail; 7. Sloth of South America; 8. Giant condor of the Andes which has a wing span of up to 12 feet; 9. The koala of Australia; 10. Komodo dragon lizard of Indonesia which reaches lengths of 10–12 feet; 11. Lion, tiger, leopard, jaguar, puma, lynx or jungle cat, bobcat and tabby-cats; 12. The oppossum, hence 'playing-possum', meaning to play dead.

MOUNTING YOUR PICTURES

Do you collect picture postcards of places you have seen on vacation? Postcards make lovely bright pictures to pin to your bedroom wall, and they look even better if you mount them first.

It is very easy to make a frame for your pictures. You will need a piece of stiff card, a pair of scissors, a ruler and some white mounting paste. The card need not be white – you can sometimes get a good effect by picking out one of the colors in the picture. Try holding your picture against different shades of card before deciding which to use.

When you have chosen your card, measure the picture and then cut the card so that it is 3 inches wider than the picture and $3\frac{1}{2}$ inches longer. Place your picture on the card so that there is a strip of card

$1\frac{1}{2}$ inches wide at the top and sides, and 2 inches wide at the bottom. Carefully paste each corner of the picture and press it down firmly.

To give your mount a really professional finish, paint or draw a black, white or colored line about half an inch from the picture all round. Use a ruler to make sure the line is straight.

When you have mounted your picture you can either pin it to the wall, or hang it from string or cord attached to the back of the mount with strong sticky tape.

Mounted pictures make good birthday and Christmas presents for your family and friends. As well as postcards you can mount photographs, pictures cut out from calendars and magazines – and, of course, pictures you yourself have painted.

Remolino and the Watch Donkey

There once lived in Spain a boy whose name was Pedro Juan Carlos Sebastian. Although he had such a very splendid name, only the schoolmaster called him that. Everyone else called him 'Remolino', which is the Spanish word for 'whirligig'.

There was a reason for this. Spanish boys have their hair cut very short all over, and this was how Remolino's mother cut his hair with her long, sharp scissors. At the back of his head, near the top, the hair grew in a kind of whirligig, round and round, and one day his father had called him Remolino for a joke.

The name suited him so well that now everyone except the schoolmaster called him that. (The schoolmaster had a very straight back and liked everyone to be called by his proper name.)

Remolino's father was called Señor Garcia, and his mother was Señora Garcia. Señor and Señora are the Spanish words for Mr. and Mrs.

As well as his mother and father, Remolino had a baby sister, one grandfather and two grandmothers and lots of uncles and aunts and cousins, so he was never lonely. But his very best friend in all the world was Burro, the old gray donkey.

Every morning, as soon as he got out of bed, Remolino would splash himself with cold water from the pump in the yard, pull on a shirt and a pair of trousers, and go straight away to see Burro in his little grass patch next to the orange grove. He would take him a bucket of clean, fresh water and in the winter a forkful of hay to munch.

In return, Burro would take Remolino for rides on his back, and together the two of them would spend happy hours wandering round the countryside.

Sometimes Burro and Remolino were very useful, for Señor Garcia would send them out to bring home a goat that had

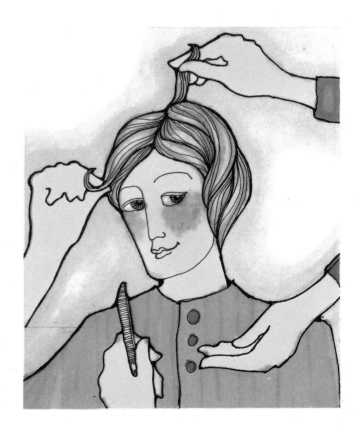

strayed. Sometimes they were naughty and would stay out too long, and when at last they arrived home Remolino's mother would be standing in the doorway, holding her hand to her eyes to keep out the evening sun, and looking for them. Then she would be cross with Remolino and send him straight to bed with only a lump of bread for supper. But she didn't stay angry for long, and soon she would come into his little white-washed room and bring him a shiny brown bowl of hot soup and some fruit, and tell him that she was only cross because she had been worried about him.

Burro did not like soup, but he was very fond of fruit, especially oranges. This was unusual. Not many donkeys like oranges because of the peel, which tastes bitter. But Burro had found a way of pulling the rind off with his teeth and dropping it on the ground, so that he could eat just the juicy fruit inside. Remolino said that showed what a very clever donkey he was. Señor Garcia, who did not grow oranges to waste them on a donkey, said quite different things. He looked after several orange groves and the family earned their living partly by selling the fruit in the market.

Once, last year, Burro had trampled down the fence that divided his grassy patch from the orange grove. He had gone to the biggest orange tree and stretched up his neck to pull down the branches. He had eaten some of the fruit and bruised and trampled a lot more.

Señor Garcia had been very, very angry. He had made Remolino fetch heavy new stakes to repair the fence, and had told him: 'If that donkey ever does any damage to my oranges again, I shall take him to town the very same day and sell him in the market place!'

Remolino had been dreadfully upset. He knew it was no use pleading with his father, who always did what he said he was going to do. It wasn't even any good asking his mother for help, as she only shook her head and replied: 'What your father says must be so.'

There was only one person he could talk to about it, and that was Burro himself. He had climbed onto Burro's back and ridden away up the dusty track leading from the house and stopped under their favorite olive trees. There Remolino had leaned forward, put both his arms round the donkey's neck, and talked very seriously into his left ear.

'Now, Burro, you heard what Papa said. You know he meant it. You must never, never go into the orange grove again, or he will sell you in the market and I shall never see you again. You might go to some horrid master who would beat you, and make you work too hard, and not give you enough to eat, and I could never be happy again without you. So, please Burro, remember – *no more oranges!*'

Burro had turned his head and looked at Remolino with wide solemn eyes and an expression that seemed to say: 'Yes. I understand. I will be good. *No more oranges.*'

And he had been good. All the weeks that the oranges had been slowly ripening on the trees, Burro had stood quietly on his own side of the fence. He had watched the fruit change from green to a glowing orange color, as warm as sunshine. He had thought slow, donkey thoughts in his head about how dull it was to eat grass all the time, and how sweet and juicy the oranges would be, and about the weak place in the fence that Señor Garcia had not noticed, and how easy it would be to . . .

Then he would think of Señor Garcia's anger and of Remolino's sadness, and he knew that the love he and Remolino had for each other was worth more than all the oranges in the world. And he would turn away from the fence and go on cropping the short grass of his little patch.

Then, one night, a strange thing happened. Remolino had just climbed into his small iron bed with the straw mattress and was counting the pale stars through the open window. He did this every night, but he hardly ever counted more than ten stars before he fell asleep. Remolino was just counting his seventh star, and sleepily thinking about tomorrow when his father had said they would be picking the oranges which had reached exactly the right stage of ripeness, when suddenly there was a most terrifying noise. It sounded like splintering wood and galloping hooves and, worst of all, the loudest hee-hawing of a donkey that Remolino had ever heard.

He leaped out of bed, just in time to hear his father shout: 'That useless donkey!

It's broken into the orange grove again, and just when the crop is ready for market! Where's my stick? He'll know about it when I catch him!'

Señor Garcia ran out of the house. Remolino raced after him. Señora Garcia stayed inside soothing the baby, who had been awakened by the commotion.

Remolino ran as fast as he could, trying to keep up with his father, and calling to him to forgive Burro just once more. But the stones hurt his bare feet, and his cotton nightshirt wound itself round his legs and tripped him up.

'Please, Papa, please,' he gasped as he scrambled to his feet.

But his father took no notice, and ran on toward the broken fence waving his stick and shouting.

All at once, Señor Garcia stopped running and stood quite still – so suddenly that Remolino ran right into him, and fell down again: Then a very surprising thing happened. Señor Garcia began to laugh. He threw away the stick, and laughed and laughed, until he had to lean on an unbroken bit of the fence to hold himself up.

For a moment Remolino thought that his father was so angry that he didn't know what he was doing, and he felt even more alarmed. But then he saw what Señor Garcia had seen, and Remolino began to laugh too.

There, in the middle of the orange grove, stood Burro, a leafy branch from one of the trees caught round his neck like a wreath, and a toppling pile of oranges on the ground beside him. Half on his nose and half in his mouth was a large straw basket which the donkey was solemnly eating. He flicked an ear in the

direction of Remolino and his father, and went on chewing.

Señor Garcia was still laughing as he turned to Remolino.

'Do you see what happened? Some of those idle lads from the town thought that they would help themselves to my oranges. They planned to sneak in and fill their baskets and get away without anyone knowing. But they reckoned without old Burro, eh, Remolino? *He* knew what they were after and he wasn't going to let them get away with it! They must have had the fright of their lives when he came charging at them out of the darkness.'

Remolino smiled proudly.

'Some people have watch dogs to look after them, but we have a watch donkey,' he said.

He put his arm round Burro's furry neck and said into his ear: 'You are the very best and cleverest watch donkey in the whole world, and I love you.'

He looked up at his father. 'Brave people are sometimes rewarded. Do you think that tomorrow, for a special treat, Burro could have just one orange?'

Señor Garcia pulled one of Burro's long ears affectionately.

'If he goes on eating that basket, Burro will have just one big pain in his tummy. But yes, I think it's only right that he should have a reward. And now you run off to bed while I put Burro in the shed for the night.'

Back in his bed, the white sheet drawn up to his chin, warm and sleepy, Remolino counted only three stars before he was fast asleep.

PARTY FARE

Getting ready for a party is great fun, especially if you can help prepare the food for your guests. Here are some ideas for party treats you can make yourself.

FOOD-ON-A-STICK

Ask your mother for some cocktail sticks. There are all kinds of food you can put on the sticks: squares of cheese, small cooked sausages, pieces of ham and bacon, raisins, grapes, pineapple chunks, slices of apple, banana and orange. You can put cheese and pineapple, or ham and apple, on one stick if you like, or arrange each type of food on separate plates and let your guests experiment with mixing them together.

FRUIT SALAD

Fruit salad is delicious to eat and very easy to make. You can use as many different kinds of fruit as you like, both canned and fresh. Peel and slice the fruit and put it in a large bowl. Make sure you cut out the core from apples and pears. If you are using cherries, take out the stones before adding them to the salad. If you are using any canned fruit you can use the juice from the can for your salad juice. If you are using only fresh fruit you can squeeze the juice out of an orange, add a little lemon juice and some sugar, and add this to the fruit.

ICE-CREAM SODA

Your friends will want something to drink as well as food at your party. Most people like ice-cream soda, and you can make it very easily. To make one ice-cream soda you will need a tablespoon of fruit (raspberries or strawberries are best), a teaspoon of sugar, a tablespoon of evaporated milk, soda water and ice-cream. Put the fruit and sugar into a glass and mix them together. Add the evaporated milk. Pour soda water into the glass until it is threequarters full, then spoon the ice-cream on top.

36

Four Brothers

There was once a huntsman who had four fine sons. When the youngest was sixteen years old they all went to him and said, 'Father, we want to go out into the world and learn different trades, so that when we come home again we can all earn a good living.'

'That is well said,' answered the huntsman, 'and I will give you as much as I can to start you on your way.'

He gave each of them two hundred gold coins and a good horse, and wished them all 'God speed'. Then the four brothers mounted their horses and rode away together.

Presently they came to a place where the road divided into four.

The eldest reined in his horse. 'Let us each take a different road,' he said, 'and in a year and a day we will all meet again at home. Then we can tell our father what we have learned.'

They all agreed to do this. They said goodbye to each other and rode away.

A year and a day later the eldest son came home. He and his father greeted each other warmly.

'Well,' said his father, 'what trade have you learned?'

'I have learned to be a cobbler,' the eldest son answered.

'That's a good trade,' said the huntsman. 'There are always plenty of shoes which need mending.'

'But I'm not an ordinary cobbler,' said the eldest son. 'I can mend anything. I say "Let it be mended" and at once it is as good as new.'

'Then let me see what you can do with this old coat of mine. See, it is worn into holes at the elbows.'

'Let it be mended,' said the cobbler, and at once the coat was as good as new.

'Well done!' cried his father, 'You have certainly spent your year well.'

Shortly afterward the second son came home.

'Greetings, my boy,' said the huntsman. 'And what trade have you learned?'

'Father, I am a thief,' answered the second son.

'Shame on you! That is a wicked trade.'

'But father, I'm not an ordinary thief. I don't go around picking people's pockets and stealing hens from their hen-roosts. I have only to wish for anything to be with me and it comes at once.' He took his father to the window. 'Do you see the hare running across that field?'

'Yes, my son, I see it.'

'Let that hare be here,' said the thief, and in a moment there it was, lolloping round the room.

'It can go,' said the thief. The hare leaped out of the door and disappeared.

Just then the third son came home.

'You are welcome, my son,' said the huntsman. 'What craft have you learned?'

'I am a star-gazer,' the third son answered. 'I watch the stars and understand what they mean.'

'But is that any use to anyone, my son?'

'It is very useful, father. When I look at the stars I can see where anything is, anywhere on earth, and I can find anything which has been lost.'

While they were talking the fourth son came in.

'Greetings, my son,' said the huntsman. 'What trade have you learned?'

'A huntsman's trade, father,' the fourth son answered.

'You're a good son, to be following my craft.'

'Thank you, father,' he answered. 'But I am not your kind of huntsman. If I see an animal anywhere that I want to shoot, I say, "Let it be shot", and shot it is.'

'Well,' said the father. 'It's nearly dark now, but can you see that hare? It's running across our field again.'

'Let it be shot!' cried the fourth son.

The hare gave a leap and disappeared.

'Where is it?' said the father. 'I can't see whether you've shot it or not.'

The star-gazer looked at the sky, where the stars were now shining. 'I see it,' he cried. 'It's behind those bushes.'

'Let it be here,' said the thief, and there was the dead hare at their feet.

'We can't sell its fur,' said the father. 'It's too torn and ragged.'

'That's because it came through those thorny bushes,' said the cobbler. 'Let it be mended!'

At once the fur was perfect.

'Well done, my sons,' said the father. 'I see that you are masters of your trades. Now we can all live in comfort.'

So the huntsman and his four sons lived together happily until one day a strange thing happened. The King's only daughter disappeared, and no one could find her. Then the King sent heralds far and wide, proclaiming that he would give the Princess in marriage to anyone who could find her.

The four brothers heard of this. 'We can find the Princess,' they said to each other. 'Let us go to the King's palace.' So they saddled their horses and off they went.

When they reached the palace they were taken at once to the King. He was very pleased to see them.

'If one of you can find my daughter,' he said, 'I will give her to him in marriage, with half my kingdom. Can you tell me where she is?'

'Not now, your Majesty,' answered the star-gazer, bowing low. 'But when evening comes and the stars are shining I shall be able to tell you.'

They waited till it was nearly dark. Then the star-gazer went out and looked up at the sky.

'There is the Princess!' he cried. 'She is on an island in the Red Sea. The island is the home of a dragon, which has carried her off and is keeping her prisoner.'

Next morning, as soon as it was light, one of the King's carriages took the four brothers to the shore of the Red Sea. There they got into a boat and rowed toward the island. When they drew near they saw the Princess walking by herself beside the sea.

'Let the Princess be here!' cried the thief.

At once she was in the boat with them. They turned the boat and began to row away.

'The dragon!' screamed the Princess. 'The dragon has seen us! It will kill us!'

Flapping its great wings, a hideous, green dragon was flying after them. It roared terribly as it came.

The star-gazer said to the huntsman, 'Brother, shoot it!'

The huntsman cried, 'Let the dragon be shot!' and it came tumbling down into the sea, dead as a door-nail.

But as it fell, one of the dragon's wings hit the little boat and made a big hole in its side. The sea rushed in and the boat began to sink.

'Let the boat be mended!' said the cobbler brother, and at once the hole was stopped up.

So they rowed safely to the land, where their carriage was waiting. They all got in, the coachman cracked his whip, and the carriage set off for the palace.

Then the four brothers began to argue. Which of them was to have the Princess?

The star-gazer said, 'The Princess is mine. If I hadn't seen her we shouldn't have known where she was.'

'Oh no,' said the thief. 'If it hadn't been for me you couldn't have got her into the boat.'

'Oh, no,' cried the huntsman. 'If I hadn't shot the dragon it would have killed us all. The Princess must be mine.'

'No, no, no,' shouted the cobbler. 'I claim the Princess. If I hadn't mended the boat we should all have been drowned in the sea.'

When they reached the palace the King was overjoyed to have his daughter back, and he listened carefully to their story.

'Well,' he said, 'you can't all marry the Princess, although you have all deserved her. But I promised her hand to the man who should *find* her, and it was the star-gazer who saw where she was. So he shall marry her. But I will give all four of you a large province of my empire, and make each one king of his own province. So you shall all be kings.

This made them all happy, and the Princess and the star-gazer were married with great feasting and merrymaking.

The huntsman was very pleased, too, for all the sons were kind to him. In the spring he lived with the cobbler-king, in the summer with the thief-king, in the autumn with the huntsman-king, and in the winter with the star-gazer-king; and so the years passed happily for them all.

MAKING MASKS

Have you ever been to a fancy dress party? It is great fun to dress up, and if you wear a mask as well nobody will know who you are! You can buy masks in most toy shops, but if you make your own you will be sure it fits in with your costume.

Masks are very easy to make. You will need a thin piece of cardboard and about 18 inches of narrow elastic.

Cut out the shape of your face from the cardboard. Then hold it over your face and lightly mark where your eyes, nose, and mouth are with a pencil. Draw a dot about an inch from each ear to mark where the elastic will be attached.

Cut out the eyes, nose and mouth—take care that you don't make the holes too big. Using a skewer, make small holes for the elastic where the pencil dots are. Tie a knot in one end of the elastic and thread the other end through one of the holes from front to back and then out at the front again through the other hole. When you are sure the elastic

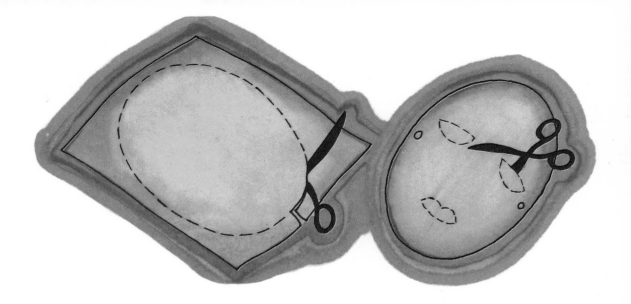

is neither too tight nor too loose, make a knot in the un-knotted end. Cut off any loose ends.

You can now draw a face on your mask and color it with paints, crayons, or felt-tip pens. If you paint the corners of the mouth turning up, your mask will look happy. If you draw the mouth and eyebrows turning down, it will look sad. To make your mask look cross, draw lines between the eyes, going down, and add some bared teeth. You could even make some of the teeth black or broken.

Next time you have a party, ask your friends to wear masks. Then you can start the party with everyone trying to guess who is hiding behind them.

43

SPRING

Spring is coming, spring is coming,
　　Birdies, build your nest;
Weave together straw and feather,
　　Doing each your best.

Spring is coming, spring is coming,
　　Flowers are coming too;
Pansies, lilies, daffodillies,
　　Now are coming through.

Spring is coming, spring is coming,
　　All around is fair;
Shimmer and quiver on the river,
　　Joy is everywhere.
We wish you a happy May.

THE EAGLE

He clasps the crag with crooked hands;
Close to the sun in lonely lands,
Ringed with the azure world, he stands.

The wrinkled sea beneath him crawls;
He watches from his mountain walls,
And like a thunderbolt he falls.

Alfred Lord Tennyson

WEATHER

Whether the weather be fine,
    or whether the weather be not;
Whether the weather be cold,
    or whether the weather be hot;
We'll weather the weather,
    whatever the weather,
Whether we like it or not.

HIAWATHA'S CHILDHOOD

Then the little Hiawatha
Learned of every bird its language,
Learned their names and all their secrets:
How they built their nests in Summer,
Where they hid themselves in Winter,
Talked with them whene'er he met them,
Called them 'Hiawatha's Chickens'.
Of all the beasts he learned the language,
Learned their names and all their secrets,
How the beavers build their lodges,
Where the squirrels hid their acorns,
How the reindeer ran so swiftly,
Why the rabbit was so timid,
Talked with them whene'er he met them,
Called them 'Hiawatha's Brothers'.

Henry Wadsworth Longfellow

The Two Iguanas

Once upon a time, in the land of Trinidad, there lived two iguanas. One of the iguanas was called Mucurapo, and he lived in a tall mango tree in the valley of Diego Martin, close to a river. The other iguana, whose name was Naparima, dwelt in the town of San Fernando, on a hill among rocks.

Living so far apart, they had never heard of each other; but, strangely, one day the same idea came to both of them—they would like to see something of the world. Mucurapo, the iguana who lived in Diego Martin, decided to visit San Fernando; and Naparima, the iguana who lived in San Fernando, thought he would travel to Diego Martin. He had heard that there were many mango trees in that green valley.

So early one morning, when the sun was shining, they both set out from opposite ends of the road that joined San Fernando to Diego Martin.

The journey was more tiring than either had expected, for they were not used to traveling. And they had not known that a great mountain range divided the country into two parts and that they would have to climb right to the top of it.

Mucurapo began the climb up one side of the mountain just as Naparima was beginning to climb the other side.

It took them many days, but at last they reached the top. How surprised they were then to see each other. The two iguanas exchanged looks for a moment in silence; then they began to talk. They explained to each other the reason for their meeting so far from home.

They were amazed to find that they had

both had the same wish to learn a little
more about their native land. As they
were in no hurry, they agreed that they
would rest together on the mountain-top
before continuing on their different ways.
They stretched themselves out, side by
side, in a cool, damp place.

Mucurapo described the tall mango
trees, with the delicious, juicy fruit on
which he lived. Naparima sighed, for he
lived among rocks and dust and had to
depend on berries which grew on the
stunted bushes in San Fernando. Both
agreed that it had been a long and tiring
journey and they were reluctant to start
out on their travels again.

'What a pity we are not taller,' said
Mucurapo, 'for then we could see both
places from here and we would know if it
was worth continuing our journey.'

'Oh, that's quite easy,' answered
Naparima. 'All we have to do is to stand
up on our hind legs and hold on to each

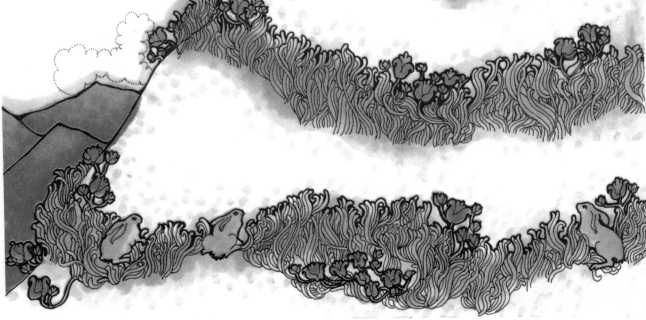

other, and then we can look at the places we wish to visit.'

'Why didn't I think of that?' said Mucurapo, who was as lazy as Naparima, and tired of traveling. He thought longingly of the green valley of Diego Martin.

The two iguanas stood up on their hind legs and placed their front feet on each other's shoulders. Their long tails gave them a bit of trouble, and at the first try they stumbled and fell to the ground.

They picked themselves up and tried again. There they stood, stretching their necks as high as they could, and clinging to each other so that they would not fall down again.

Mucurapo turned his nose toward San Fernando, and Naparima turned his nose toward Diego Martin. But the foolish creatures forgot that when they stood up and stretched their heads their hooded eyes lay at the back of their heads. So although their noses pointed in the right direction, their eyes looked at the places from which they had come.

'Good gracious!' exclaimed Mucurapo. 'If only I had known that San Fernando looked exactly like Diego Martin, I would never have traveled this long distance!'

'But Diego Martin is exactly like San Fernando!' cried Naparima. 'What is the use of going on?'

The two iguanas stood there, swaying, for quite some time. Then Mucurapo complained: 'You are treading on my tail!'

They fell to the ground and looked at each other.

'What a waste of time and energy!' exclaimed Naparima.

The iguanas bade each other a polite goodbye and set off the way they had come, back to their homes again. And to the end of their lives they believed that Diego Martin and San Fernando – which are as different as different can be – were as like as two peas in a pod.